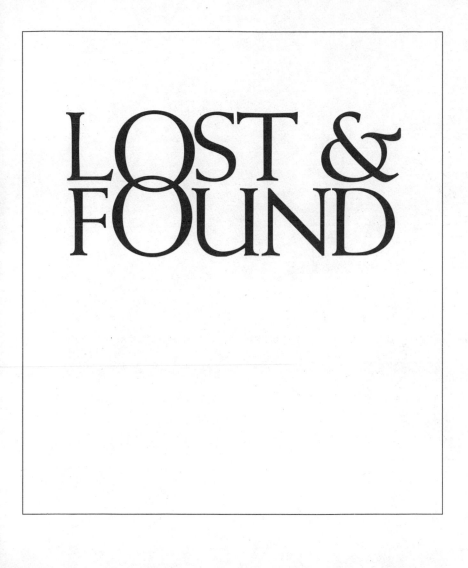

LOST & FOUND

Finding the
Silver Linings
in Life

JOHN A. JENSON

HYPERION

New York

A Special Thanks to: Lacy Reeves, Mark Sanborn, Joe Howard, & Debbie Vargo for contributing their time and expertise to this project.
Design: Robert L. Schram, Bookends Publication Design
Editor: Barbara McNichol, Marcom Services
Originally published by Putt-Putt Publishing

Library of Congress Cataloging-in-Publication Data
Jenson, John A.
     Lost & Found : finding the silver linings in life / John A. Jenson.
          p.   cm.
     Originally published : Broomfield, Colo. : Putt-Putt Pub., c1997.
     ISBN 0-7868-6481-8
     1. Loss (Psychology)—Quotations, maxims, etc.   I. Title.
PN6084.L57J46   1998
155.9'3—dc21
                                                           98–23329
                                                              CIP

FIRST EDITION

10   9   8   7   6   5   4   3   2

To my Mom and Dad

My best friends

and

my biggest fans.

Thanks!

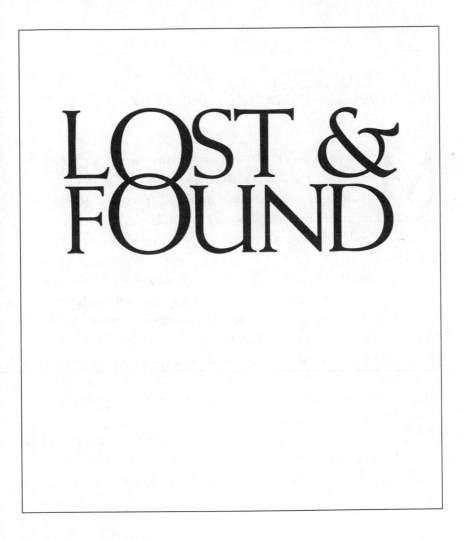

In the 1920s, he began making his mark on this earth.

M
Y GREAT UNCLE JOHN built a white two-story house to live in and a big red barn to work his crafts. He planted trees for shelter and used the pond nearby as a place to reflect. This man who set out to build an enduring farmstead ended up instead producing memories that will last a lifetime.

One Saturday long ago, my father and I took a trip to the farm. Eight inches of sparkling white new snow in the farmyard enticed me to make my best Pete Rose slide into an imaginary base. My father disapproved of my antics, and pointed at the snow I had just "wrecked." But during the time we were inside visiting, the wind came up. And as we said goodbye to Uncle John and walked to the car, I now pointed to the place where I had "wrecked" the snow.

There were no tracks, no marks, no evidence we'd even been there. Everything was smooth, and so was my remembrance of that beautiful day. Something about the peacefulness and serenity of my uncle's farm has forever left a lasting impression on my mind.

Uncle John must have felt the same way. At 85 years old, he wheeled his chair and a bag of art supplies a quarter mile to the road where he sat to paint a portrait of the mark he had made on this earth. He painted his farmhouse and barn as if he were giving them a fresh spring coat. The cottonwood trees in full bloom towered over the yard, and in the emerging clouds, a subtle silver lining which depicted his outlook on the day.

My uncle's portrait of his farmyard hangs prominently in my home today. And though I LOST my Great Uncle John when he was 102 years old, I FOUND inspiration in realizing that ordinary people can significantly impact the lives of others.

I have written this book to share my impressions of what I've *lost* . . . from my childhood to my life in the business world . . . and to look at what can be *found* in our deep search for answers.

—JOHN A. JENSON, 1997

I LOST

my little boat

as it slowly drifted away.

❋

I FOUND

the importance of staying close

to the things in life I cherish.

When friends wander away from our lives,

it doesn't happen all at once.

They're like the sheep that get lost

by nibbling their way from home.

I LOST

my pet turtle when

he walked off into the distance.

❋

I FOUND

he was headed toward water,

not away from me.

When it comes time to make a move,

make sure we are seeking opportunity

and not escaping unfinished business.

I LOST

my shovel when it got buried

in the sandbox.

✻

I FOUND

if we dig a little deeper,

we find what's important.

This is true in relationships

as well as in sales.

The treasures we find are

seldom on the surface.

LOST & FOUND

I LOST

my favorite ball when

I kicked it on top of the school.

❄

I FOUND

an abundance of balls when

I figured out how to get to the top.

Prosperity awaits those

who have purpose

in what they do.

I Lost

my mobility when

my baby-sitter put up a fence.

❄

I Found

that the fence wasn't to limit my movement

but to keep me safe.

When we look back at our past with open eyes,

we lose sight of what happened

and begin to understand

why things were done certain ways.

I LOST

faith in the new boy

who brought toast for Cub Scout treats.

❋

I FOUND

empathy for him after learning

he didn't have a mom.

Looking deeper into

a person's circumstances

leaves room for compassion

in a time of doubt.

I Lost

the handling of my bike

when my dad took off my training wheels.

❄

I Found

that those same training wheels I relied on

had limited my progress.

I've had people in my life whom

I relied on for a time.

Upon breaking away, though,

I realized they had really been holding me back.

I LOST

the skin on my chin

when riding my bike cross-handed.

❄

I FOUND

that taking a risk isn't always the best idea

when I'm racing at full speed.

We should always
be looking to improve,
but not when
we're "on a roll."

I LOST

my grip on the monkey bars

while swinging from one bar to the next.

❄

I FOUND

that, to be successful,

I had to let go of one rung

before latching on to the next.

I've ruined several relationships

by failing to let go of the old

before bringing in the new.

Being suspended with nothing to hold on to

is a scary feeling.

I LOST

the feeling in my hands

while trying to fix my skis

in sub-zero weather.

❄

I FOUND

upon getting his help, that my dad

either had great circulation

or the world's warmest heart.

This example

of unconditional love

is especially remarkable

considering I told him

to hurry up the entire time!

I LOST

the "handle" of a catch

I should have made.

❄

I FOUND

that a "big head" from previous catches

got in my way.

Holding on to past successes

keeps our hands full . . .

and us full of ourselves.

I Lost

the game when the basketball

went off my foot and out of bounds.

❄

I Found

the value of taking responsibility

for my own actions.

People will respect us

for owning up to our own mistakes . . .

in my case, especially when there was nobody

within 20 feet to blame it on!

I Lost

my position on the basketball team

due to a poor attitude.

❄

I Found

that sitting on the bench

didn't make it any better.

Controlling our own attitudes

is a choice.

Attempting to change the attitudes of others

is a project.

I LOST

faith in my team's ability to succeed

when I wasn't there.

❄

I FOUND

that they could win without me.

Life is full of humbling experiences.
Once we realize everything
doesn't directly revolve around us,
it takes the pressure off.

I LOST

my scorecard

somewhere on the golf course.

❄

I FOUND

that everyone in my group

knew exactly what score I had.

I'm *always amazed how people*
don't pay attention to our lives
until something directly affects them.
Then it's all very clear.

I LOST

my breath when a deranged classmate

tried to choke me with a chain.

❄

I FOUND

a shocking realization that

not everyone deserves to be trusted.

It takes time to build strong relationships

when we've had bad experiences.

We breathe easier when we surround ourselves

with people we trust.

I LOST

my way while exploring

a neighborhood unfamiliar to me.

❄

I FOUND

that asking for help

got me back on track.

It's been said our greatest attribute

lies in our ability to show vulnerability.

When was the last time we asked for directions

and someone turned us down?

I LOST

my favorite tree in our back yard

as a result of a lightning storm.

✻

I FOUND

a view of the golf course

I never knew existed.

If we only made an effort to

look beyond what we see every day,

it wouldn't take a loss

to improve our vision.

I LOST

my favorite teacher

when she moved out of town.

❄

I FOUND

there were other people

I could learn from just as well.

Changes in people and circumstances

are a major part of life.

Our success depends on our openness

and adaptability to change.

I Lost

a coin in the parking lot

of the supermarket.

❄

I Found

my money and eagerly

looked for more.

When we have a victory,

we immediately search for another.

That's why we should constantly create successes

for ourselves and those around us.

I LOST

touch with dear friends

when I left for college.

❄

I FOUND

fresh perspectives with

each new relationship I developed.

Although stepping out

of our comfort zone is difficult,

it expands our horizons

in many ways.

I LOST

my friend and brother

to marriage.

❄

I FOUND

an addition to our family

I can count on in time of need.

Our selfishness will resist

changing situations or relationships.

We must put aside our fears

and make way for more in our hearts.

I LOST

touch with a very special

person in my life.

❄

I FOUND

a renewal of warmth

in our recent reunion.

It has been proven to me

that true friendship

is not contingent upon

constant communication.

I LOST

a self-improvement kit

that cost me $600.

❄

I FOUND

that the spark I needed

didn't come from inside a kit

but was within me the entire time.

LOST & FOUND

We find ourselves searching

through books, tapes, and channels

for something to ignite us into a world of bliss.

Obtaining information is great,

but it's up to us to act.

I LOST ·

the motivation to

finish the project at hand.

❄

I FOUND

that I was still motivated . . .

but to do something else.

My motivation to spend a day

lying on the couch is sometimes so strong

that nothing gets in its way.

I have little choice but to give in.

I Lost

my cover when my Halloween mask

got ripped off my face.

❄

I Found

I felt more comfortable when people

knew me for who I really was.

Only a few fortunate people

will ever see us for who we really are.

Cherish them,

for they are our true friends.

I LOST

a significant portion

of my hairline.

❄

I FOUND

all of a sudden, how important

the rest of my hair became.

LOST & FOUND

We don't always realize

how important some people are

until we are in danger

of losing them.

L O S T   &   F O U N D

I LOST

respect for my brother Russ

when he seemed happy about

losing his wrestling match 18 points to 2.

❄

I FOUND

that, after he'd been pinned 22 consecutive times,

"winning" to Russ was simply

finishing a match.

My favorite definition of leadership is
"someone who has the ability to surpass himself."
Knowing ourselves and our capabilities
allows us to find victory even in defeat.

I LOST

sight of my goals

when they appeared unattainable.

❋

I FOUND

that reaching toward my goals

had stretched me in many ways.

I *was once told what's important*

is not necessarily attaining our goals

but enjoying who we become

in the pursuit of them.

I LOST

a contract that would have

kept me busy for months.

❄

I FOUND

some time to figure out

what would keep me happy for a lifetime.

Our outlook on day-to-day tasks

is fair-to-partly-stagnant.

Forecasting our futures

is what makes life meaningful.

I LOST

my enthusiasm when

I wasn't acknowledged for my contribution.

❄

I FOUND

the importance of recognition

in all that we do.

They say the fragrance stays with

the person who presents the rose.

More important than receiving appreciation

is noticing what others do well

and using those opportunities to praise them.

I LOST

my drive when

I thought I had "arrived."

❄

I FOUND

that news of my arrival

had not been sent

to those who kept on moving.

Complacency is

a one-way ticket to

the back of the line.

I Lost

fair and square

at another person's game.

*

I Found

that, if I really want to win,

I need to make the rules myself.

M_y friends will attest that

it's difficult for them to win at games I create;

the guidelines tend to change midstream.

Life is no different.

Only we ourselves know if we're ahead or behind.

I LOST

valuable time after deciding

to take a sure-fire shortcut.

❈

I FOUND

that, in life,

there is no such thing as a shortcut.

L O S T & F O U N D

An acquaintance of mine tried

just about every get-rich-quick scheme known to man.

But taking shortcuts to success

has only left him short on his cut of the cash.

I LOST

my identity

while under the influence.

❅

I FOUND

that, the more I altered myself,

the less of me I became.

It occurred to me one day

that since I am the only me that will be,

I had better present myself in

my best possible light.

I Lost

my courage to sit by the swimming pool

when I wasn't pleased with my body.

❄

I Found

myself sitting next to a guy

who was missing part of his.

No matter how bad we think our lives are,

someone else's life is worse.

The troublesome part is it often takes that realization

to make us feel better.

LOST & FOUND

I LOST

some weight in an attempt

to get my life together.

❄

I FOUND

it takes more than weight loss

to feel better about myself.

The changes

we make to our exteriors

don't always transfer within.

I LOST

at my first attempt

at living away from home.

❈

I FOUND

it said more about

the positive environment at home

than it did about me.

We have to stop beating ourselves up

for any temporary lapses in strength,

remembering that failure

is a short-lived event and not a person.

I LOST

my roommate

when he moved out of state.

❄

I FOUND

how much I enjoyed

my privacy.

The first step to happiness

is learning

to live with ourselves.

I LOST

sleep by sweating

the small stuff that takes place

in day-to-day activities.

❄

I FOUND

that life is

mostly small stuff.

Dale Carnegie writes about

a tree on Long's Peak in Colorado

that, for hundreds of years,

survived avalanches and lightning strikes.

It was eventually brought down

by a host of small beetles.

I LOST

my vision of

the person I wanted to become.

✳

I FOUND

that, by clarifying my values,

my vision reappeared.

Helen Keller said,

"Worse than being blind

is being able to see but to have no vision."

I suggest we create a vision

that is consistent with who we are.

I LOST

all regard for someone

who caused me pain.

❄

I FOUND

understanding of a person

whose background was

different than mine.

Longfellow once said,
"If you were to read the
secret histories of your enemies,
you would find in each man's life
sorrow and suffering enough
to disarm all hostility."

I LOST

the audience's attention

when I took too long to make my point.

❋

I FOUND

that, the more I talk,

the less I have to say.

A great quality in a person

is taking time to be brief yet understood.

I agree with the famous writer who said,

"If I had more time,

I'd write a shorter note."

I LOST

my place and stopped speechless

while presenting to a large group.

❄

I FOUND

that, surprisingly,

the world didn't come to an end.

Whether speaking to a group

or living life in general,

the best advice I ever got was,

"If you lay an egg,

stand back and admire it."

I LOST

my fortitude

when I entered a room

full of people I didn't know.

❄

I FOUND

the wisdom to ensure that

none of them would be

strangers again.

Most of the trees lost in Hurricane Andrew

were not native to Florida.

We are stronger in our own environment

but need to continually expand it.

I Lost

some revenue

when I decided to donate

my services to a non-profit.

❄

I Found

a sense of gratitude and appreciation

that money cannot buy.

I know what Dr. Calvin K. Fercho meant

when he articulated the stages of our lives:

"There's a time to learn,

a time to earn,

and a time to return."

I LOST

control of my car

when I didn't see the upcoming obstacle.

❄

I FOUND

that, in some cases,

it pays to go "looking for trouble."

Identifying where

problem areas exist

is the first step to overcoming

or avoiding potential barriers.

I Lost

my cool when I realized

people weren't interested in what I was saying.

❄

I Found

by taking an interest in other people,

they responded differently.

Dale Carnegie said,

"You can make more friends in two months

by taking an interest in other people

than you can in two years

by trying to get them interested in you."

LOST & FOUND

I LOST

my tolerance

for certain people's incompetence.

❋

I FOUND

the easier I could overlook it,

the more I was above it.

George Eliot said,
"The responsibility of tolerance
lives with those who
have the wider vision."

I LOST

respect for the furniture salesman

who had all the answers.

❋

I FOUND

how much more effective he would have been

had he asked the questions.

The TV detective Columbo

always got what he wanted

by doggedly asking

questions of others.

I Lost

a client

over a little misunderstanding.

❋

I Found

that, in the eyes of any client,

understanding is everything

and nothing is little.

The client is not always "right."

But that doesn't mean

we should call any "wrong"

to his or her attention.

I LOST

my nerve

to walk into an office

and make a cold call.

✻

I FOUND

that, if I acted courageously,

people perceived me that way.

The phrase "fake it until you make it"

has never been a favorite of mine.

But I learned that the closer I get to my fears,

the smaller they become.

I LOST

a client when she questioned

my commitment to quality service.

❄

I FOUND

an opportunity

to prove how important

client relationships can be.

It's like being behind in a game

and having to play twice as hard to win.

Two things end up happening:

the victory is sweeter

and we learn how to prevent the situation

from happening again.

I LOST

a job

when my principles differed

from those of management.

❄

I FOUND

how good it feels

to go down swinging

for what I believe in.

Roy Disney said,

"When your values are clear,

decision-making is easy."

I LOST

a mentor

when I moved out of the state.

❅

I FOUND

how lucky I was

to have had someone

pushing me to be better.

The world is full of people

who tell us what we want to hear.

It's better to align ourselves with those special people

who tell us what we need to hear.

I LOST

my favorite tie

when I left it in a hotel room.

✳

I FOUND

that, once I got over it,

I immediately had a new favorite.

The great things in life

we could never live without

are quickly forgotten

and often easily replaced.

I LOST

confidence in myself

when my sales were down.

❋

I FOUND

that looking back on successes

starts the rebuilding process.

Although we can't spend our lives

living in the past,

reminding ourselves of our accomplishments

gives us momentum for the future.

I LOST

my belief in the earth's goodness

when my town

experienced major flooding.

❄

I FOUND

that, when Mother Nature

is finished with her destruction,

Human Nature takes over.

As flood waters rise,

so do the contributions

of people in the community.

I LOST

a strange-looking plant

as I pulled it from my garden

early one spring.

❄

I FOUND

I had missed out on enjoying

a spectacular late-blooming flower.

We tend to lose confidence in others

before we give them

the time or encouragement to blossom.

I LOST

appreciation for an exceptional man

when, on first meeting, he seemed so normal.

❄

I FOUND

I felt gratified knowing

that extraordinary people

aren't much out of the ordinary.

I *love the idea of great people*

wearing ordinary shoes like we would wear.

When we're comfortable being ordinary,

we've arrived.

I LOST

sight of why

I was put on this earth.

❄

I FOUND

the peace that

only solid faith can give.

I'm convinced it's not what

we lose in life that's important

but what we gain and where we look

in our search for answers.

I Lost

sight of a friend

while mingling at a party.

❄

I Found

how special people are to me

when their absence is apparent.

When we enter a room,

does it get brighter or darker?

Does the energy level go up or down?

Or, when we're not in that room,

are we missed?

I can tell you that my Uncle John is missed.

A FEW CHRISTMASES AGO, members of my family sat around the kitchen table reminiscing about the man and the farmstead he so lovingly built. We decided to take the 40-minute drive to the countryside and see his farm again. The 40 minutes, though, unexpectedly turned into an hour. We wondered if we were lost. When we finally stopped the car, I stepped out onto the road to look around. I had a sense that this was the very spot where Uncle John sat and painted his farmyard portrait many years before.

I couldn't believe my eyes.

There was no house, no barn, no trees. Just like the tracks I had made in the snow many years before, there was now no evidence Uncle John had ever lived . . . except for his farmyard portrait and the loving memories he left behind.

Upon reflection, I believe this is his legacy:

The marks we try so hard to make in life

will eventually be lost.

But the impressions we make

on the minds of others last forever.

LOST & FOUND: IMPRESSIONS

I Lost

I Found

LOST & FOUND IMPRESSIONS

I Lost

I Found

LOST & FOUND IMPRESSIONS

I LOST

....
....
....
....
....
....
....

I FOUND

....
....
....
....
....
....
....

LOST & FOUND IMPRESSIONS

I Lost

I Found

LOST & FOUND IMPRESSIONS

I Lost

I Found

LOST & FOUND IMPRESSIONS

I Lost

I Found

JOHN A. JENSON credits his ordinariness to his North Dakota childhood and a laid-back Colorado lifestyle. Through both the spoken and written word, he uses life experiences to bring simplicity and insight to a much-too-complicated world. In his profession as a trainer and speaker, John helps people look within themselves to reach a high level of effectiveness.